# all blue so late

# all blue
# so late

poems

Laura Swearingen-Steadwell

NORTHWESTERN UNIVERSITY PRESS

EVANSTON, ILLINOIS

Northwestern University Press
www.nupress.northwestern.edu

Printed in the United States of America

10   9   8   7   6   5   4   3   2   1

Library of Congress Cataloging-in-Publication Data
Names: Swearingen-Steadwell, Laura, author.
Title: All blue so late : poems / Laura Swearingen-Steadwell.
Description: Evanston, Illinois : Northwestern University Press, 2018.
Identifiers: LCCN 2017031340 | ISBN 9780810136342 (pbk. : alk. paper) |
    ISBN 9780810136359 (e-book)
Subjects:  LCSH: Teenage girls—Poetry.
Classification: LCC PS3619.W436 A78 2018 | DDC 811.6—dc23
LC record available at https://lccn.loc.gov/2017031340

*for Justin*

CONTENTS

# Fourteen

You don't know what an unreliable narrator is,
but you will learn: No one in the future is on your side.
There are ghosts in my brain that you haven't even met yet,
stories I have yet to tell anyone. There are specters
that fester and worsen the longer I wait to pronounce
their names. Why he left. What happened passed out at the party.
Said *stop* in the hostel. The needle dangling from his corpse
when I refused his friendship. My cousin stealing Phillip's
violin to sell for crack. The times I almost said yes
or did say it, desperate to be held, for love, for shelter,
for a roof or a meal or safety. This begins now, girl.
This is all you—your awkward curls, your in-between body—
and I'm the monster: I don't want to spare you any pain.
I want the unbroken woman you will be to exist.

# Moebius

I'll tell you all my secrets.
I love it when the black man wins—
at the polls, on the charts, when he makes it
to the end of the movie. I say *he*

not because my father has his face;
he's just as close as the screen lets me get
to myself. My father has a crush on Martha
Stewart; my mother isn't into white guys.

I once loved math: the balanced equation
proved destiny, justice, romance—but
I got caught in the brambles of language
and now I have to make my own sense.

Today I soaked and cooked pigeon peas,
browned the sugar, fried the poultry,
added coconut milk, stock, and spice.
I wanted to make something beyond me.

My friend once concocted this dish
for a lake woman from Michigan.
The flavor was deep as the well
that sustains your family, whole

as the globe that taught you where
you come from. I don't come from
there, or here, this Brooklyn building
of brick, smoking spots, bike racks,

and a full-color block print tag
that says MOEBIUS on one wall.
When I see it, I want to be
a mathematician again.

Why didn't that happen? Was it my skin?
Too black? Too thin?
Too composite? Unparalleled?
Infinite as a cloud.

If there was a day I learned I was black,
I've always known since then.
Neither my mother nor my father taught me
pelau. The day my friend cooked it,

I didn't know the work. How heavy
to haul those ingredients home.
The hours to allow it to simmer
slow. But in that vapor, in the heat,

my names brown, steam gold.

# Caldera

Eight hours standing, stocking beer coolers
before the local men shuffled in after work,
brown and worn from building in the sun,
or windburned, caked with ocean salt. I wiped fat
off the cylinders of the hot dog machine until
I smelled metal; made change; spoke to anyone:
the man who bought a Klondike bar most afternoons,
the girl who brought Tupperware of tuna *poke*
her mother made to sell. Mostly I was alone.
When I was sure they'd all gone home,
I flicked the lights and the locks.

I turned my back to town and walked
along stone walls studded with hibiscus and palms,
all blue so late. The street radiated fever.
The misanthropic sea hissed. Space grew long,
polishing its dark blade, stars two thousand nicks
on its edge. The old volcano beckoned me
to burn my loneliness, to sacrifice my sorrow
to the attic of the sky.

# Building the Quabbin

Because strangers in a city miles away thirst,
will thirst, the flood fills the bowl of our valley,
erasing destinations, swallowing
the meaning of roads.

           The water's clear as air.
Clean through, our towns still exist in low tones
beneath a hundred fifty feet of drinkable ore.
Those were houses, a post office, a school,
a church

      it took seven years to unmake,
for the water to weep

          all the way up, droplets trilling,
keening through manmade gaps in rock.

When they are stronger, what they want
becomes a weapon. Something as simple as
what keeps you alive.

# Fourteen

The past is a horror story still haunting the present—
you just don't know it yet. But twice a week, third period,
American History corners you. Ms. Mostoller
patrols the classroom armed with questions with no right answer:
*Laura, did Nat Turner help the abolitionist cause?*
You guess yes: he was an ex-slave, he led a rebellion.
You haven't done the reading, so when Ms. Mostoller tells
the class the epic of a murderer, a psychopath,
you can't argue. *Turner incited violence that hurt*
*those still enslaved the most.* You haven't done the reading, but
you know the need to remind the enemy they bleed too.
You're a kettle on the verge of screaming, you don't know why.
You haven't found the language. Ms. Mostoller hears you sing
in the choir, once. She compliments your clarity of tone.

# Necropolis

Out of town, down
along the cliffs and walls
sunken in surrounding earth.

Ahead for miles, the villages, farms,
vineyards, the gentle hills of Umbria,
gold and orange, soaked in open sun.

A switchback path led me down
among trees, where darkness pursued
its thousand shadows.

Two women took admission.
They expected no visitor
so late in the day, or the season.

Up a little hill,
red globes hung from a tree,
otherwise bare:

lanterns of a kind. No,
pomegranates, full and fresh.
The flesh of one, fallen,

gave easily. Elsewhere,
I might have taken one to eat,
but here I couldn't stomach it.

More orbs dangled above me,
seeded hearts bright against
the mesh of greens ahead,

the mounds of grasses, weeds,
and mosses that had made a life
smothering the ancient stones.

Down, and the grass brushed my knees.
Down, beneath my breasts, down, level
with my sight—then I went under.

The tombs were measured,
with wide paths between them.
They gaped—besides the occasional

spider's web splayed in a corner.
Tons of stone leaned together
to shelter the dead.

Each small and careful cove
impressed the air in its own way,
but all had pallets meant for bones.

*They look like benches in a sauna,*
I thought—and I sweated a little
to see. What was there to fear

but the silence? But the silence.
The faintest trail of cars growled
on the road not so far away,

and birds' eveningsong above,
but I felt silence

as I leaned my head into
the archways of tombs
and saw darkness.

In some, the structures
of barracks or bunkers lurked.
Or little windows let light in

from the opposite wall. I made out
plants, ferns curling, feathered strands
groping the stone towards earth.

But in one doorway, looking in
was like going blind.

So I looked at everything else:
ice green lichen.
Aggregate, calcified white.

I found traces of writing
chiseled into the stone. Clean.
How clean the lines.

# processional

he lifts my grandmother's body

   a sheaf of reeds
he picked himself, cattails
rustling in the wind

     he carries her

as though he meant to make something
useful, to weave a basket,
to give those bones the benefit
of new intention.

      this is what they mean
when they say *good man*: they mean
a love strong enough to smile
as though he could lift her anywhere,
carry her down the aisle

      with my father
and the other white-gloved men.

# Fourteen

They call you *Steadwell*, after your older sister. The kids
who know you from elementary school. The gym teacher
who warns you, smiling, sharing earrings transmits AIDS, who says
seated ladies cross their legs. None of them tells you the *why*
of anything. They hoard their knowing looks and won't say why.
You chafe at the burden of legacy, the chain letter
of your genetic code. Someone forged your signature, you
don't know why. A star is erupting. You think it might be
your sister. She sabotages your plans, screams in your face.
You belong to her less each day, less the baby gazing
up, waiting on her grace to fall. It hurts to look at her
directly. You can't touch without searing. You only touch
when she goads you into attack. You spin wildly through space,
broken satellite doomed to orbit her unstable star.

# Sakura

Sculpting cherry blossoms reminds her of home,

threading, twisting copper wire through rose quartz.
Her hands burn with the memory of spring

flowers storming the Tidal Basin,
dragons perched along the riverbank, shedding
pastel scales. Valentines. Ghosts

dissolving on an outstretched tongue.

# In the Orchard

Because I was told: in countries I don't know
there grow orchards of apples ancient and wild,
an abundance of dreamfruit christening the trees,
strains alien to here, purple, blue, of such rich flavor
a tongue could catch the sugar on the air,

because the sun was so intent on me the summer
ruby millipedes marched in armor around the roots
while I harvested reptilian avocados,

because I watched him breathe
one afternoon, his arms flung back
in the daffodil glow of my room,

I know one reason it hurts so much to live:
there are places on this planet
sweeter than any heaven.

# When the Man Talked Around Me, When He Talked Over Me

Then he became a fish swimming backwards.

And the lantern fish mimicked a beacon.

A lighthouse built too far inland, a building

of trapdoors and stairways to nowhere.

Observe, if you will, his absence of meaning.

Once I followed a ghost through a decade of night.

*In the world of men, I sewed my tongue into a stone and grew small. It was how to survive. I removed vertebrae as a parlor trick. I sawed off my feet and sanded my limbs down gradually, an inch or so at a time. I whittled my breasts and hips away. I sewed my tongue into a stone where it shriveled and curled, desiccated, the frond of a fern. Soon I was so tiny, I could be carried around in a shirt pocket. Food costs were down. But I wanted to be smaller still. I wanted to pass through the eye of a needle. Before long, even atoms loomed over me. I was good at my job. Very good at my job. You'd be surprised how easy it was.*

# Fourteen

It all goes down in the cafeteria, the warehouse
where throngs of wild children congregate,
jostling for space with their gangly bodies, their plastic trays,
trading jokes, rumors of hookups, fights, suspensions, the news
that matters. Everyone sits with their own: the mostly white
table, kids from Southeast, basketball players, the black girls
with good grades and no white friends, the kids whose infant English
still wobbles. Your chest rustles with broken glass as you scan
the tables, hungrier than you've ever been. If only
you had the look (Hoyas Starter jacket, hair ironed flat),
the markers of belonging—but you want to be the star,
the one whose life goes nova. The standout. Look at you now,
standing alone among hundreds of people. Nowhere girl
hunched over her food at an empty table. Don't look up.

# Cafeteria Tech

The woman we ignored as kids, except to mock the curious hairnet
    gridding her head, the woman gloved and dressed in white
like a nurse, full-bodied, with reasonable shoes, bands of fluorescent light
    gleaming in her working face, and her certain lipstick set

in a straight horizon line—or frowning with resolve, never unkindness—
    brusque but generous, the woman whose work we ridiculed days
the spread disappointed us, but too often neglected to praise
    when we loved the food, when it brought us joy, made us buoyant

as angels (if not as good)—she cared. She nurtured us, rough and small.
    Didn't she teach gratitude, and grace? Didn't she feed us all?

# The Woman Pouring Handfuls of Ash

isn't the title
of a painting
by Vermeer,

it's only me
dumping a cache
of cigarette ends

in the trash.
I emptied each
butt of purpose,

smoked them
until red singed
the root, watching

a canal of white
Midwesterners
herd small dogs,

monster strollers,
and fashionable facial
hair along the block.

My teacher once asked me,
*Why are you so angry?*
her laugh loud and round,

although it's clear
anger owns a warren
in her too,

that the feeling
is as home to
her as honey.

She could tell.
*Teacher, I'm angry*
*because people*

*ask for it*, I don't say.
I moved to this city
and my rage matured:

it's strong, bitter beer
that's steeped
inside me years.

Dark nights I want
to stalk bars to find
somewhere to

pull blood
from the mouth
of a fool

of a man
bigger and slower
than I am,

crush the seeds
of his teeth
against my bones.

I long to tear this
world apart
like rotten fruit,

starting small.
I long to bloom
a riot in a dive;

I measure
the distance
between

the edge of the bar
and the skull
of a stranger.

I watch myself reach
for the bottle
I'll crown him with,

violence as proof
of survival. My teacher
asked to see

if I knew the truth:
*why* is as simple
as reading the news.

# If it helps,

count the number of bullets lodged
into the faces of buildings, the skin
of furniture. Measure the trajectory and fall;
collect the empty shells.

If rewinding helps,
lean close and squint

to watch the flower break loose
from the man, collapse, the torn
ecosystem of skin and neuron,
the final organ sigh.

Our inevitable
endless dead
echo and echo again.

# Fourteen

Shelley struts the blacktop trumpeting *not guilty!* the day
the Simpson verdict is announced. Black people win for once,
we get away with murder. You are the generation
stamped *superpredator*, tried as adults, condemned to life
by men like Mark Fuhrman. The cops who beat down Rodney King
lurk unchecked in your streets, while politicians who commute
into your city blame your music, your video games,
your neurochemistry, your parents' moral fabric, *you*,
for ruining the neighborhood. Shelley struts the blacktop
in loose jeans, loudest girl in the grade, maybe the smartest.
She code-switches better than anyone you've ever met.
Shelley who won't shut up, even in class. She knows herself,
afro puffs fuzzy and bold. You slick your hair back with gel
each morning. It freezes stiff, not a hair on your head free.

# Last Composition

It took decades for you
to grow so small, shrunken
flower, withered branch,
all the blood gone out of you.
You've become a winter river,
Mother, so blue, age spots
daubing your skin. Breakable
hands, your mother's ring.
I place my hand on your spine
and cradle your cold face
close, your silver-gold hair
clinging to my chest. I slide
one of your nude bras
over your fallen breasts. Joyous
nipples, still so young, frosted
pink. I push you into place,
lift you, relieved at the cold
solid teeth of the clasp,
relieved, too, to be done
with that moment, to let
your face fall away—
but for the first time, I notice
your eyes, night deserts, granite
eyes beyond. I'm dressing
you in forest green, Mother.
I need some buffer
between myself and the blank
frosted message in your eyes.
Here is that soft, long shirt, then,

that made you soft, too, good
to hug, although I rarely did.
As I pull it past your head,
your hair springs wild,
the only part of you still unruly,
still electric, antennae curling
and clambering over each other
to touch me.
I force myself to look
at your face again. Your mouth
hanging open so I can see
your fillings glinting, the fragile
yellow of your teeth, whitish
tongue, your little lips. Small
blue pepper of the nose.
The careless folds of skin
at your throat. Your whispering
brows. I lower you slowly,
taking your right wrist,
still soft, your hand a crumpled
paper in my fist.

# Sandusky Bay

I was sleeping when we passed your house
It was late—you were sleeping, too

In the middle of the water
In the middle of the night
    on Sandusky Bay

suddenly the floating train

Far away the street posts
brandished hot fruit over cars

It was too dark to see
the rust and bolts that made the bridge

only lines of light and the inlet
the wavering of you

# Fourteen

Your body announces itself during a long blizzard
that drapes D.C. in powder. The air blurs white, the enthroned
land threatens to swallow you. You enjoy the challenge. You
and your friends trudge the neighborhood drifts, one house to the next.
This is the longest snowstorm of your lives. Time realigns.
How every tree and house and road you know renews itself.
While your friends are nestled in at Sherrie's, eating pizza,
playing Super Nintendo, a door opens inside you.
Red badge, velvet ladder unfurling from your center. How
cool you sound, sharing the news. You discuss the change softly.
Each of you has questions, anecdotes whispered woman to
woman: now you are one. It's getting late. Light is leaving.
You swaddle yourselves in damp layers against the new wind.
Gauze moon at the heart of winter: now the whole world is blue.

# To Love Men Is to Love What Can Kill You

The sociopath blasted the song "Girls" on repeat,
Ad-Rock's thin tenor wrapped around my wrists
like wire as we tore through the city in his Jeep.
In murderous nightmares my sister and I sprint,

cornered by an enemy in the red-light district,
dismembered on Amsterdam's cobblestone altar.
Stored in the brain's amber are clots of insects
presumed extinct; their descendants

hibernate decades, then barbarian over the fields
to pulverize everything living and green.
His silver eyes nailed to the dashboard,
the sheets: I tried to remain still as a seed.

# Fourteen

Michael from homeroom won't leave you alone. He skulks after
class, by your locker. Short Michael asks, *What race do you like
better*, then invents his own answers. One day after school
he has a secret. You bend an ear to his mouth—the coil
of his tongue slips in. Bonfire of shame, fury—but later,
you'll relish recounting your war story to the others,
their scandalized shrieks. But all of you have stories. Marlene
sat in one boy's lap and felt his dick get hard—and one day
at recess, another grabs her tit. She yells as he runs,
but she doesn't really mean it. Boys swarm her. They decrypt
invisible text in her smile. A few years back, you'd sleep
at her house on a weekend night, squinting at scrambled porn
until your eyes hurt. Secrets. You two made one of your own.
Now she dances ahead, sure, desire feathering her back.

# Shadowing Vesuvius

In a Neapolitan museum, allegorical paintings: the veneer of painted skin has
worn away from some of the bodies, leaving them skeletal. Structural. The
artful slope of one fibula stays with me.

In Rome, an obscure Franciscan crypt displays a regulation habit in a glass case,
minuscule Bibles, and a few paintings of notable friars. At the exhibit's end,
an elaborate celebration of human mortality, one monk's passion. He sculpted
cartloads of bones into chandeliers, stacked them, piled skulls, decorated the
ceiling in whorls. A few posed figures, after centuries, still wore a layer of
desiccated flesh.

And I in awe as though
the candle of myself
had dimmed.

# Fourteen

Some things you do excellent well. Lithe as an animal
or avenging angel on the field, the organs in you
gushing energy out to your legs: glory to the thighs
and calves propelling you, feet rocketing the soccer ball—
quick as a nimble little forward, your long lunge rivals
a keeper's ample reach. This sport favors the in-between
build, the nerd-jock switch. People come from countries, and brown is
an international color. The sunlight paints you dark.
You sprint until lean, until your pores weep salt. Sharp autumn
air stings your nostrils and lungs. You yell at the refs, muscle
opponents aside. Your allies wear your stripes, and you know
the enemy's name. Deemed most valuable when you go wild
between the lines, in real life, don't be a bitch, or a beast,
too fast, too strong. Hide the fact that you're feral all the time.

# Charleston // Squaw Valley

each tree here a woman who died
with an answer

                                                        *in the bowl of green*
                                                        *I grew young again*

a pine standing sentry, fur
crown and mantle

                                                        *I carried my sorrows*
                                                *I cleaned them and shelled them*

the ones from the old ways
in tanned hide and bone

                                        *in the thin air gasping, bewildered by cold*

and the women who knelt in the
apse of a city

                                        *light of the morning how could you take me*

each woman who died
left behind her a question

                                                        *could we have saved them*

a stain on the air

                                                                *a stain on the air*

although aspens kept flashing
their white semaphore

no one could decipher the leaves

# Valentine (Up Top)

At Cedar Point, I become American again—
which is not to say I'm not still black.
I'm with four grown friends, all black,
unabashed about it—but innocent, just
children again, milling among Midwestern
families, camps, teams. Neon, inordinate,
screams from visors, fanny packs.
T-shirts with insulting logos
soak with sweat,

but everyone's united in the sun
and ululating dream. June. Afternoon.
Swings, hills and loops, flashing
games, plush prizes, foods sweet salty fatty,
we squeal our delight and surprise, want

to know the deeper meaning
of names: *cobra, teacup, millennium.*
We laser tag and mallet immortal gophers,
giddy for golden tangles of funnel cake,
foamy flavored ice, for fries steeped
in chili, bacon, cheese—all in,

grown as we are, older arteries
and bones, we ride. Shift our vision. Uplift,
the will to live rising to a clean high note.
The impassive lake shimmer and spinning
toys below. I have known

such fear. I have known fear
of the body, of the beloved, of my own magic
brain, my soft wild heart. The pure fear
should it end all wrong, the good work undone.

Come evening, the lights click on,
and we transform, purple and blue.
The garish fluorescents fade,
the clashing roller coaster tracks
darken, the bitter mix of pop songs
mutes to its core. Look. Talk soft.
It's only us, now.

# Fourteen

Never been to jail. Never held someone you care for deep
inside. Never watched your sister Bekah sneer and side eye
normativity. You aren't yet the brazen you'll become,
a rogue bolt of white staining your curls. You've never witnessed
your father weeping, your mother's sigh unfolding like silk
when she retires. You haven't seen Courtney and Kate flower
in the rainstorm of your nephews, never met Aliah.
You will dirge at your grandfather's deathbed, hear the dolphins
singing each to each. The world has yet to reveal itself
in the soft seal of a woman's thighs tight against your ears.
Look to the clay, to the microphone, and ink that bleeds black.
Harness the charge in your sorrow: the vast oceanic
that tangoes itself together and apart, the waxing
unknowing. Grow patience to build. Acceptance of breaking.

# Patrick

The entire Spanish language almost went to hell

along with the Hendrix canon

after the summer our church group built a home

for a family in Virginia.

As we worked, the curvy goth daughter glared,

porcelain and black.

I struck hesitant lines on the tar roof to show

where the tiles should go:

pluck of a string, a puff of smoke, and a blue chalk mark

spun loose, a simple arrow

to the other side. Sun lingered in my skin months after

that summer, months spent missing

the nights we circled the picnic table, sand castles and wind

groaning on the boombox,

longing rolling through me like a stone. You checked my grammar

once I got familiar: *That's cómo está*

*to you.* To me, you had the body of a man, muscle threading

in your endless skin. That fall,

the noose. The loss. And my first ghost.

# Genre

When I almost fell out of the world, Christina grabbed my arm like we were in some action movie. I mean: I made my life an action movie, or a sordid drama costarring a redhead and a bustier. Rather, we told ourselves a joke: three poets and a lightbulb.

My ex wept and wept, I mean he simply would not stop. Nothing could stanch that sad, and my blood wanted to fall out of my body. So we went on a buddy adventure without each other, he to the desert, I to an island in the middle of the Pacific. I thought I was the diva in a tragic opera, but in hindsight, it was a one-panel comic. Or chick lit. I was, after all, a Woman Making Her Way.

Still, I wanted to fall out of the world. My mother came to visit, but left me bildungsromaning under some mango tree. Then Christina came, which might have turned my life into a fairy tale, only the third fairy never arrived to save the day.

Before the big reveal, you should know: This was never an erotic novel. Christina and I hiked to a nude beach, where she showed off the neat fluff of her New York pussy, the cultivated cunt to my feral thatch. Those whiskers whispered to me, and Christina grinned like she had made *decisions*. I wanted to make decisions again—my own, bigger than a razor and falling out of the world.

Not an erotic novel, but a hotly contested feminist tract. Or a Bible story revolving around a woman and a burning bush. It was time to get back to it, to tell the tale. So maybe you were the third fairy, Dear Reader, the part of the prophecy that brought me back to—

# Fourteen

You're staring at the ceiling Sunday morning when your dad
announces it's time for church. Without moving, you say no.
Disappointment in the way he shuts the door. The latch sighs
and his footsteps murmur darkly to themselves. Your parents
have begun to give up. You are a sullen carousel,
silent, grey—your family steers clear. You stain your walls blue,
the darkest shade your mother permits, hibernate for months.
This is your life: The autumn you're faithless, and always cold.
Your ponytail freezes. The leaves will not stop changing. You
are posted at the bus stop, you are constantly waiting
on the chance to adventure to a miraculous world.
You hoard your imagination and longing notes to self.
You know someday they'll read them all, realize your genius.
But you're unearthing a solitude that stays. It remains.

# Where I Lost

Late night, it was better to stumble drunk
the half mile home from the train

than to wait on a fickle bus in a downtown
that went dark at night—not so dark that

no one was around—or exactly that dark;
I didn't wait to see what anybody wanted.

I crossed into the empty lot by the college
where high-hanging flowers diffused the light,

towards the lake that beckoned
beyond rushing currents of cars.

I could sprint across all six lanes, but after
seeing a white girl get bumped by an Impala

a block from there, I walked the underpass.
It reeked of shit. A man sometimes slept

on the waterlogged cement, swaddled in clothes:
I had to shuffle past him to get home. I knew

artists hid there too, the man tickling his sax,
wailing over a small boombox looping Muzac,

and writers who bloomed the tunnel walls with script
the city painted over once a week. Afternoons,

light filtered through the grates, grey and cool, and noise—
as though Oakland were humming as she braided her hair.

The water unfurled, nature's flag. At dusk,
it shimmered beneath bulbs strung on wires.

Night herons kept watch along the circumference,
wary, crests slicked back. Vines spiraled the girth

of arches and columns that flanked the flush of trees
hiding Children's Fairyland from view, the park

where the burlesque dancer with hot pink hair
donned wings to play with kids on Sundays.

She danced freelance, with one regular gig
in the city. She looped the golden lasso of her

grin around your shoulders when she invited you
(who were mine) to watch. Your reddening read *yes*.

A truth that naked could embarrass only you.
The lake itself, that isolate jewel,

twinned with a roaring traffic swarm. Bless the hot rods,
the coots and the grebes bobbing and weaving in ink,

myriad of miracle birds bejeweling the lake
with plumage du jour. Beauty will make you forget.

But cop cars prowled our block like sharks,
and a sidewalk shrine waved a weary balloon

where a bullet met the body of a boy.
He might have been one of the kids hanging

on the corner constantly, who heckled you
mercilessly, called you Elvis, ran game, said

you had no right to me: *White boy go home.*
The bullies buffeting your skinny body

in grade school had never left, I knew—
but when you pounced, snarling nonsense,

I held your rigid body back with newfound fear.
The boys cackled, goading on and on . . .

We hid in the dive bar after work, challenging
the goldfish in their slimy tank to sad staring

contests at the end of each month. At the end,
you wept into my lap. I stared, blank as the pint

I couldn't drink fast enough, and you confessed
all these years you'd hated this place. The home I chose.

I pored over maps with hope, researching parks,
punk rock bars, succulents fat in desert patches,

the bounding cold of the Pacific where seals
slipped between shoals and sheaves of seaweed,

places I thought would feed your wonder,
would make you happy as a transplant.

I thought the lake would be enough, to each day greet
the extended family of pelican and goldeneye,

cormorant and tern. To admire the live oak,
the tea tree curled under run-on sunlight.

I even loved the smoldering corner boys,
even when they brought the edge of pain

directly to the pupil. Blossoms on the margins
of the road. You once brought me armloads

of prehistoric lilies, a bundle of children
leering, listing, dominating my entire day.

They're still my favorite flower.
The city is, too: it taught me to walk

with keys for claws; it splashed my laugh
with sheer color. Maybe you couldn't love

such mystery, so *other* than what you knew.
Too late one night, stumbling home alone

along the lake, I saw a puffin
in the water, large as a toddler

wading in the shallows, its plumage stark white,
a fascination I ran home to share.

We couldn't find it in any of your guides. But
I know it was there. I thought you believed me.

# the dead black girl doesn't care

what we call the dead black girl

the dead black girl is a daffodil on the table
    wrapped in newsprint

the daffodil is dead also, decomposing in a black
    trash bag

the dead black girl is abandoned on the curb
    we put her there

even you—who tells the legend
    one black girl whispers

to another to prevent
    our own vanishing

# Church and State of Being

Praise the man's breath warming the gun barrel.
Praise the woman's hands cradling pills like jewels

longing to revert to ore inside her. Praise the wrist
its gaping locks. So much is impossible to say—

so praise the immolating monk who shocks
the passion insomniac in us, the moon's bright hem

stitched into our brains. She names her own poison.
He twists the noose with his own hands. The body

drinks the needle, and the blade. Once I drank
until phantoms crowded the edge of my vision,

black waves throbbing with syntactic light. If I moved,
my organs would collapse. I ached

with want
for a door.

If freedom means
owning one's own life,

praise the desperate ones
who shred and rend, who call forth

the shriek and the bang, the shatter
of the world unwanted.

Praise the girl who knew no way beyond
ordinary horrors, who doubted

it was enough
to offer

of her mouth
what breath

a flower might sip
without notice.

It is holy, and so small,
the decision to live.

# Fourteen

Vinyl pants from the punk rock store will make you cool. Promise.
Learn the way you always do, knowing nothing, even what
they mean. Wear them baggy, with battered steel toes. Your father
spits *you look like a hooker*; you don't know why. You're a year
away from losing your virginity; you don't know how.
Almost every night, a shouting match interrupts dinner:
your father, your sister, your brother, sometimes you. Someone
storms away from the table. Someone's feelings are hurt. Soft
as a suckling pig that knows it's built to be stuck—you scream,
cut back as regular practice. It's right. It's only fair.
You need to learn to fight, to quickly wound, deflect, disarm.
You learn this early, as the stranger child, the smaller child.
It is not a lesson you want. You haven't mastered it.
You will. Decades later, it will never feel like triumph.

# PechaKucha for Suicides, Seekers, and Ecstatics

### marijuana

I learned the rudiments of philosophy from the disembodied heads of Guevara and Marley, our noble dead. Lifted on smoke clouds like an angel, I observed the arguments of men. Each night, the boy I wanted to marry drove me the long way through the park, and deer lit the dark with isinglass eyes.

### cocaine

Hunger created us. Earth rotates and revolves, light bombards us, magnetism and gravity tease our hairs, our skin shucks cells and regenerates, our words and gestures wail with electricity. *It takes all the running you can do to stay in the same place.*

### methamphetamine

Cartilage collapses like an ill-built igloo, a sin against the face. Bodies soak in homemade sores. Driving through Bakersfield, a demon minivan ran us off the road. Once I tried to reconfigure my teeth, using my fingers.

### LSD

Sophomore year, we acted as animals do, giddy with it, especially the day the little redheaded girl fed us paper before Spanish class. We glowed and so did everyone, all us beasts with radioactive fur and daynight vision. No one learned but laugh.

### mescaline

He purred and leashed and led me. Why: he kissed like rain. He cooed my face in his long fingers as though Joni Mitchell had taught him love. The whole menagerie of music crowded and bowed to him, and he read my hidden thought like his own invention.

### ecstasy

When you learn joy is a mechanical byproduct, you salivate on cue, *love me, lust me, like me*, let it fall to flame and laugh it up, *lap me, lust me*. A man of mine once broke his brain by eating too much E.

### opium

Heartbreak smoke-blue, scimitar-sharp, aching every morning for a year, a pink carnation bruised against my overbite. I tended silence, spied on mountains. What a tragic cartoon short. He awoke on ice; he forgot what had warmed him. I didn't: I did.

### crack

When you're struck by lightning too many times, only scorch matters. How frightening those chalky beasts, loping zombies in the gutter. We feared them less for the harm they might do, and more for their mirror of ache and desire.

### heroin

Vomit fell out of us like snow. We inhaled poison our bodies couldn't loose, then retched pointlessly behind the bushes in the yard. It felt. Spirits crept at the corners of our vision. Holy Book we swore this was real, we were dreaming.

### mushrooms

No light but that of the moon—it marked blue highways. We drove through ghost town business districts, Portishead playing. Our car stopped in the suburbs. We walked down beach and into ocean, not hesitating, even when Orion shot a comet from his bow.

### tobacco

Any second can be sacred, if you take it. We honor our breath by stunting and pruning it, each five-minute break a bonsai garden to explore silence inside. We honor exchange with strangers, the blaze and small talk freely given. We honor the outside, the eternal expanse of open air.

### alcohol

Juniper, barley, potato, malt, wheat, grape, hops. Poison all exalted, cover me in fuck, black the night out: remembrance trumps remembering. Tonight, I'll tell you everything you think you want to know.

# Submerge

Kim called himself a primitive (my mother would have called him *rough*). We shacked up together on the banks of Lago de Atitlán, an old volcano now sunken and filled with water. No one knew the depths of the lake, but it was said a monster lived inside. I believed it. At night, moonlight carried on the shuddering surface with its tongue hung out. No one local knew how to swim.

We perched naked on a boulder until flushed with sweat, then he dove cleanly into the deep. I stared at the haunted water. When I was full enough of fear to leap, hands first, my vertebrae clicked backwards at the impact. That was the beginning of my body's old age, another story.

I sustained a moan for hours between actual earthquakes, as the little volcanoes left around the lake complained. Kim built us breakfast of fresh rolls, avocado, and sea salt, while I stared at the water, pen in hand. He sang little Danish tunes. He kissed me and murmured, *Sometimes you make me shy*.

Kim showed me where light couldn't reach. He introduced me to my body, then he took it. When I was almost all belonging, almost sold, he whispered the killing word in my left ear.

So I learned the line
between the seasons
of my heart.

# Valentine (Underground)

*What do you see in the hearts?*

Sparks travel
between a couple.
The woman clutches
a metallic chocolate shop
bag, and another packed
with red tissue.

A pink envelope stamped
with tread marks where I wait
for my train. I smell the bouquet
crackling in plastic as a woman
rushes past me to get home.
I watch someone watch
a violinist through her phone.

*Why does today feel long?*

Red clothing seems important,
and I look close for loneliness.
When I think I see it, I almost cry,
*I'm lonely, too! On my commute,*
*I sometimes lean long into*
*strangers like you—*

but I'm headed for a late dinner
in lipstick and an Outfit.
I should've stayed home

with my books. I should be
beefing up my verbs.

A woman on the train
tucks a lingerie tote under
the bench with her feet;
I walk poorly in these heels.


### How do you know you're cared for?

My date is taking me to dinner,
and I think we'll kiss,
we will, and I know we'll try
to bring our bodies together.
What should I want,
besides meatier verbs?

I want the little boat of me
untroubled by strange
humans I encounter on the train.
The woman ranting to no one,
the man fixing the errant lace
in his loafer. So many lonesome
people here. Or just alone.


### Where will you fly?

When I look up again,
all the lovers have gone,
the woman with lace, silk, or satin,
the couple clutching decadent treats
(the man's mouth swollen
pink from kissing).

I know I'll kiss my date tonight,
smear his lips with mine.
I hope to want

to kneel before him,
baffled and grateful
that love is a wild wonder,
that it is unfathomable,

that even the lonesome
are occasionally granted
the wide curve of its beak.

# Fourteen

Your life becomes secret, even to you. The cigarettes
you explore one furtive stolen moment at a time. Dream
Tupac Shakur is kissing you, fanning your cheeks with long
eyelashes. Jewelry, clothes slid into your sleeves and backpack
in the no man's land of department stores. Your confusion
when a friend strokes your back until you drip with hot honey.
Your sister's boyfriend visits your house, a bouquet of musk
and cologne. You have a crush on everyone, long to be
overwhelmed. You steal your father's worn copy of *Delta
of Venus*. Your first kiss, then kisses trickle in barely
quickly enough. You begin sneaking pulls from your parents'
liquor cabinet when the house sleeps. You drag razor blades
the length of your forearms, leaving sad irritated welts,
carving your initials. Now you begin to write poems.

# heat and the sirens return

the birds but come from us,
high   sharp and hollow-boned

o violent flute     sorry litany

    brute herald

o shark at the end of the

world   shark
    with abacus eyes

a high school teacher in Chicago
in Baltimore, a mother

    wait to read

letters in the blood we float

# So the bell rings

and I'm chasing an ice cream truck in high holy want, blaring at
the top of my lungsful for Chipwiches but craving a snow
cone, really—not the kind manufactured and wrapped in plastic,
but fresh-scraped scooped and soaked with color, *really*
saturated color, dripping like a little mango, seriously new-fallen
mango impatient to shudder free from its skin, like me some
days, a little round sun to swallow, really *that's* what I want, to
swallow the sun, I want it burning the perfect into me, a dart of
diabolical beauty, yes, I want it inside me really and truly enough
to run wailing down the street from top to bottom, oh darling, ice
cream trucker, mine O mine I want it for real, I'm coming for you,
I'm after my *joy.*

# The Long Walk Home

My mother, merciless with grammar,

had me reading long before

I learned to tie my shoes.

Perhaps that's why

I've always mistrusted

straightforward kindness.

I'm waiting for the trap to spring, skittish

as anything furred and built of meat.

Maybe that's the reason I keep walking away

from this poem: you are impossible.

You follow me down wells, across the blackened plains.

When I stop breathing, you pump my lungs yourself.

I snarl, *Go away! I bought this pain,*

only to earn your enviable smile.

Now look what you've done, stroking my hair that way.

My solitude becomes intolerable

and I sigh at the creeping vines.

# Fourteen

When Jill's punch sinks into your stomach, fold. She'll walk away
and never bother you again. When Michonne brandishes
a cane, strikes—hold her. Use your height. Use the muscle you earned
playing sports, the tricks your older sister slipped up your sleeve.
She won't be the last to try to hurt you. Most are women
or girls who once loved you, whom you disappointed. These two
hate you for your advantage, your luck. They call you *princess*.
Jill comes from a mining town in West Virginia. She drawls
and calls herself *redneck* for laughs. Michonne lives in the hood,
in a part of town known for drivebys, for gang violence.
These girls know the world much better than you. Jill knows meth burns
boredom and misery into oblivion. Michonne
knows brown girls count for nothing, that Spanish makes her lesser.
They know they can never really hurt princesses like you.

# Orvieto

Stone underfoot, overland, swaddling clothes of stone, from the bulge of the cobbles to the rough shimmers along facades. A gondola dangles in the air.

The city is slowly sinking. The young are leaving for prospects down the hill. Businesses are moving to the underground mall. The Etruscans who once settled here dug into the soft volcanic soil to build tunnels, wells, and pigeon coops. Much of this is still intact, as are their ancient tombs.

*It's never been so quiet*, I think, before the clock tower hammers twice. As though the town itself can hear me, the ghosts from ancient wars. We live in their hospitals, play music in their churches, explore their crypts; they want some notice. Ana Badia lifts fallen lettering from the cemetery: she honors these gravestone serifs by making art. Her husband is uneasy with this: that is his reverence. When the issue arises, they stare at each other, then change the subject. Marriage suits them.

My heart is buried, the rest of me worn down by constant excavation. It's never been so dark as in the Badia bathroom with the broken switch before I flick my lighter and find my way.

I wanted to bring
you with me this November.
But I brought this back.

# 22 Antrim Street

The blue front door with three diamond windows.
Worming brown and gold shag between the toes.
Plastic-wrapped furniture clutching bare legs.
The bowl of assorted nuts, calm in their shells;
silver-jawed tools to crack them to the meat.
The glass-topped table for cards and drinking.
The recliner with a crank to make it slump.
The fly-green cut glass dish of glossy candies,
like pillows striped with white, red, and yellow,
facets glittering. The insides of a geode,
good to look at. They were purses of desire:
we always craved them. But we always knew
the same sweets had been there year after year,
draped in an imperceptible layer of dust.

I don't remember any of this. Not the strange
bathroom softness. The poodle cozy drooped
like a question mark on the toilet paper roll.
The cover sprouting erratic turquoise dreads,
the cushion beneath harassing through one
irritating split in the plastic. The shocking
green mouthwash, alien, I'd never seen before.
I swigged from the bottle once, relishing the sting.
Like staying under in the swimming pool, or holding
my body to task through overwhelming feeling.

I don't remember the smell of aftershave—
my grandfather's brand—I knew from each time
I saw him. He always bent his cool face
to kiss us. The scent persisted, staining our skin.

Before and after. Where the game played out.
A throng of people clustered around the screen
with the fake wood panel. The TV tables
they propped up to eat their meals. The low couch,
dark leather, that swallowed even grown men.
A crowded room, a small one we never played in.
The jaundiced lamplight too faint. The shows stark blue
on the faces of the grown-ups. Ghost blue.
They stared with their eyes burned out. They stared
at my grandfather in that room. Too late.
He couldn't even talk. He was plugged into
a hanging bag that looked like water. It wasn't.
He seemed as though he saw us. How could he.
Nothing was as simple as it looked.

# Power

*1*

The story can't be found in the face of the man—
though somehow it's always a man

who knows his hardware, current, and spark,
who learns from other men how to build.

Although the face is where dreaming begins,
the craft comes from the careful hands

stripping wire to its copper, threading charge
from battery to switch or timer to invent a circuit—

circuits useful to us as constellations were
to navigators in past ages, or conquerors.

Useful as fertilizer, or a bundle of nails.
Watch his gradual hands

attach the detonator.

*2*

It takes
such care
to clean

to bathe
with cloth

to swab
the rail

to scrub
the recoil
spring

the barrel
the joints
oiled

just as a man
cleans
his child


### 3

To gather up the body's salt
and dust. To compact stone
until the story breaks free.

I hold the blade
    of grass in my mouth.

I read the black glint
    in a woman's eye.

I leave behind the riot of ghosts,
    walk the branching roads.

Build the merciless language.
Polish the chrome until it sings.

# Fourteen

This year you surrender without notice, take forty blue
pills on a whim. You're waiting for death when the boy you like
calls. You change your mind, tell your mother. Her face is on fire
all the way to the hospital. Time collapses itself.
You sip charcoal and vomit like a champion. They say
there's no lasting damage, but they're wrong. Something is broken.
The woman who carried your being burns in the hollow
you abandoned. Ghost daughter. Phantom pain permanently
blues the irises bent toward you. She leans over your bed
the way she used to every night when you were small, tucked in,
rapt in a story embroidered with colorful voices,
intrigue, emotion. Your mother's tears swelled at bittersweet
endings. She held the illustrations up for you to see:
the Selfish Giant's long body shrouded in white blossoms.

ACKNOWLEDGMENTS

The following poems first appeared as listed below, with a few changes. I'm deeply grateful to these editors for their support.

"Caldera" first appeared in *The Cortland Review.*

"Building the Quabbin" first appeared in *anti-.*

"Necropolis" first appeared in *The Collagist.*

"processional" first appeared in *RHINO.*

"Sakura" and "the dead black girl doesn't care" first appeared in *Vinyl Poetry.*

"If it helps," first appeared in *pluck! The Journal of Affrilachian Arts & Culture.*

"PechaKucha for Suicides, Seekers, and Ecstatics" was featured on the podcast *Talus, or Scree.*

"So the bell rings" first appeared in the anthology *Learn Then Burn 2.*

# GRATITUDE

I have so many to thank. I am so lucky for that. These are folks who directly helped this book happen, sometimes just by reminding me who I am, as a person and an artist both:

Rick Barot. Eleanor Wilner. Nathan McClain. Angela Davis Fegan. Omoizele Okoawo. My family, for being the ones I can always come home to. Kenyatta Rogers. Khary Jackson. Kim Johnson. The Detroit School, all of y'all: Vievee Francis, Matt Olzmann, Nandi Comer, Tommye Blount, Airea Matthews, Aricka Foreman, David Blair, and Jamaal May. Bakar Wilson. Ven Smith. Chas Jackson. Heather McHugh. A. Van Jordan. David Haynes. M Mark. Gregory Pardlo. Maya Marshall. Jericho Brown. Patricia Smith. Andy Thigpen. Rob Sturma. Toi Derricotte and Cornelius Eady. Christina Olivares. Evie Shockley. Martha Rhodes. Taylor and Brenda. Reginald Dwayne Betts. Diana Hall. Stevie Edwards. Ricardo Iamuuri. Mahogany Browne. Tyehimba Jess. Larry Pawlicki. Bill Bennett. Joanna Robinson. Thank you for bringing me light and love every day, Tom, when working on this book has sometimes been so damn hard.

Thank you to Callaloo, the Community of Writers at Squaw Valley, the Kentucky Women Writers Conference, the Frost Place, The MFA Program for Writers at Warren Wilson College, the Rose O'Neill Literary House, Black Nerd Problems, and Brick by Brick.

Jacqueline Jones LaMon, Anne Gendler, Parneshia Jones, and Northwestern University Press, thank you for your generous, relentless eye. Cave Canem, I can't believe how much you have given me. Thank you for teaching so many of us our worth.